BE THE BEST AT
BASKETBALL
JOHN ALLAN

CONTENTS

www.hungrytomato.com

First published by Hungry Tomato Ltd in 2021
F1, Old Bakery Studios, Blewetts Wharf, Malpas Road, Truro,
Cornwall, TR1 1QH, UK

Copyright © 2021 Bright Bound Ltd

ISBN 978-1-913440-05-3

A CIP catalogue record for this book is available from the
British Library.

Manufactured in the USA.

Picture credits:
(t=top; b=bottom; m=middle; l=left; r=right; bg=background)

Shutterstock: alphaspirit (back cover); Andrey_Kuzmin 31bm;
FOTOKITA 1bg; mejorana (all top tips bubbles); mhatzapa 6mr,
8tr, 12tr, 15tm, 23br, 26tr, 28tr, 32tr; New Africa 31tm; Timolina 31ml;
Ververidis Vasilis (front cover).

Every effort has been made to trace the copyright holders, and we
apologize in advance for any unintentional omissions. We would
be pleased to insert the appropriate acknowledgments in any
subsequent edition of this publication.

Disclaimer: The author, publisher, and bookseller cannot take
responsibility for your safety. When you attempt any of the
exercises in this book, you do so at your own risk.

INTRODUCTION

Lightning quick and loaded with skill, basketball is one of the world's most popular games. Its style, atmosphere and million dollar superstars make it a fantastic spectator sport, and millions of people tune into games in America's NBA league every week. But it is a great game to play too, and we want this book to inspire you to get out there and shoot some hoops!

GUIDE TO SYMBOLS & ARROWS

Throughout this book you will find helpful illustrations to show you how to do a drill. Unless specified, the lines and arrows are used to represent the following.

To help you understand the terms in this book, we have used the following...

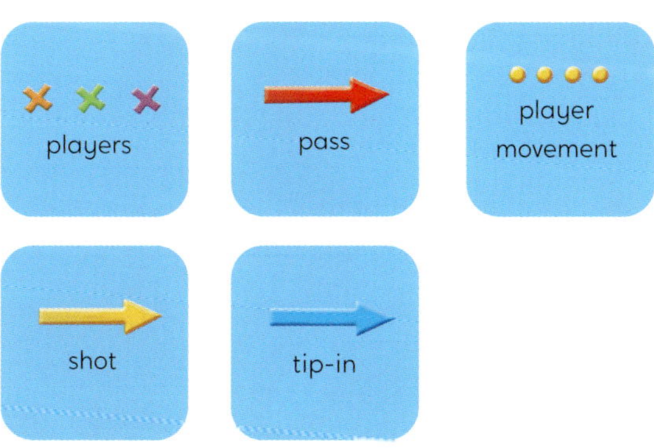

DRIBBLING

You are not allowed to walk or run while holding the ball in basketball, which makes dribbling one of the first skills to be mastered. It is not only important to keep the ball under control and away from opponents, but also to do it at speed.

BASIC DRIBBLING

While you are dribbling, at least one foot must stay in contact with the ground and you can only use one hand at a time. And remember, once you have stopped with the ball you must pass or shoot; you cannot start dribbling again.

STEP 1

Do not look at the ball, keep your head up so that you can see the other players on the court.

STEP 2

Using your fingers and your wrist, push the ball downwards and slightly ahead of you with a clean, smooth action.

STEP 3

Allow your fingers and wrist to move smoothly up and down with the ball. Do not let the ball make contact with the palm of your hand, feel it with your fingers and shift it with your wrist.

STEP 4

As you move forwards, bend your knees and keep your body over the ball to shield it from opponents. Always dribble with the hand that is farthest away from your opponent.

STEP 1

As you dribble across your opponent, stop suddenly on the foot nearest them. Remember to keep the ball away from your marker.

STEP 2

Turn your body back the other way, pivoting (see page 8) on the foot nearest the marker. Keep your back turned to them to shield the ball.

REVERSE DRIBBLING

When there is an opponent in your way, you can beat them by stopping, changing hands and dribbling away in the opposite direction.

STEP 3

Keep turning until you are facing the opposite direction. As you bounce the ball at the end of your turn, collect it with your other hand (now farthest from your marker) and continue play.

TOP TIP

The reverse dribbling technique must be executed in one quick, smooth motion to outsmart your opponent.

ON THE COURT: DRIBBLING

Practice your dribbling with these simple drills, designed to improve your ball control.

DRIBBLING REACTION (2–6 PLAYERS)

This drill is great for helping you to learn the most important rule of dribbling; look forward and not at the ball.

STEP 1

Players dribble the ball in a standing position, looking forward at a coach or another player standing a several feet ahead.

STEP 2

When the coach or other player raises their arm, the players stop dribbling, that way the players must be looking at them to know when to stop.

PROGRESSION

Instead of dribbling from a standing position, walk and then run with the ball towards the coach.

DRIBBLING CONES (1–10 PLAYERS)

In a match situation you will not be dribbling in a straight line very often!

Set up a line of cones, placing them about 2 feet (0.5 meters) apart. Then simply dribble in and out of them using one hand. Start off slowly, then speed up. As you improve, try switching hands. You will find this makes dribbling through the cones easier.

DRIBBLING TAG (2–10 PLAYERS)

This drill teaches you to protect the ball while you dribble.

Simply mark out an area just big enough to contain the number of players. Each player has a basketball which they must dribble continuously. While dribbling and protecting their own ball, they must also try to knock the opponents' balls out of their hands. When a player loses their ball or stops dribbling they must leave the area. The winner is the last player left dribbling the ball.

TRAFFIC JAM DRIBBLING (3-15 PLAYERS)

This drill is good for all dribbling techniques, because it requires you to keep your head up, change hands and speeds, and protect the ball all at the same time.

STEP 1

Three or more players (each with a basketball) stand in a circle, ideally around the center circle. Players must dribble in a straight line to the other side of the circle, all starting at the same time.

STEP 2

Then they will all converge in the middle as they pass through the center of the circle.

STEP 3

Only by cleverly dribbling the ball through this 'heavy traffic' will they make it to the other side.

TOP TIP

If you have enough players, make the circle two or three deep so that when the first players have made it through, they can pass the ball to the next set of players and go to the back of the line to wait for another turn.

BALL HANDLING

Basketball is so quick, it is crucial that as soon as you get the ball you get it under control and keep it well protected from the opposition.

CATCHING GRIP

This is the grip favored by pro basketball players. Place your non-shooting hand on the side of the ball, gripping with your fingers, while your shooting hand is positioned behind the ball, with your palm facing forwards. This makes either passing or shooting an easy option.

shooting hand

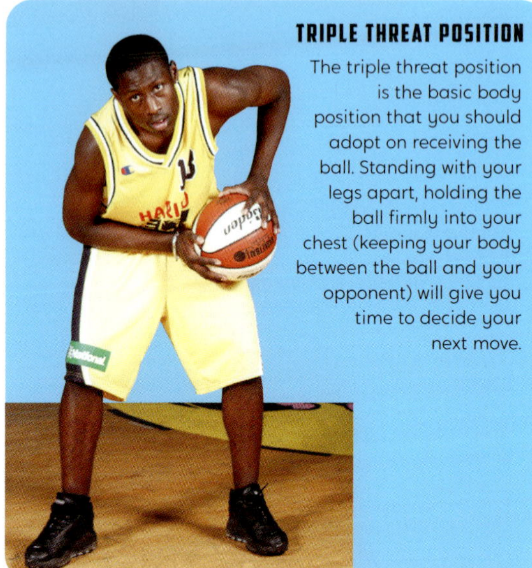

TRIPLE THREAT POSITION

The triple threat position is the basic body position that you should adopt on receiving the ball. Standing with your legs apart, holding the ball firmly into your chest (keeping your body between the ball and your opponent) will give you time to decide your next move.

PIVOTING

When you stop with the ball, you are allowed to change direction – as long as you do not move the foot on which you stopped. This is called pivoting, and you may want to use it to turn and 'square up' to the basket.

STEP 1

Once you have decided to turn, lift the heel of your pivot foot up and shift your bodyweight over it.

STEP 2

Lift your non-pivot foot up and begin to turn your body round, using short steps for balance.

STEP 3

Keep your knees bent, your back straight and your head up. When you complete the pivot, you should end up in the triple threat position again.

STRIDE STOP (HALF STOP)

When you catch the ball in midair, you are allowed to take a step to stop. Using the stride stop allows you to stop legally, and it can also be used at the end of a dribble.

STEP 1
Move towards the pass, stretching your hands out and keeping your eyes on the incoming ball.

STEP 2
As you catch it, step forward with your leading foot. This becomes your pivot foot and counts as a step.

STEP 3
Bring yourself to a halt with your second step. You should end up in a balanced triple threat position with your head up and your knees bent, leaving you ready to pass or shoot.

JUMP STOP

The beauty of the jump stop is that it only counts as one step, so you can choose either foot as your pivot foot.

STEP 1
Jump towards the ball with both feet parallel.

STEP 2
Catch the ball in midair, then make sure that you land with both feet touching the ground at the same time.

TOP TIP
After completing a jump stop, and once you have pivoted on one foot, you cannot switch to the other.

PASSING

The easiest way for a basketball team to keep possession of the ball is by passing it, and it is also a much quicker way to move the ball up the court than dribbling. There are three main types of pass to choose from, depending on the game situation, your position on the court and that of your teammates and opponents.

CHEST PASS

The chest pass is the safest and most accurate pass in basketball, but it can only be made when you have a clear path between yourself and the pass receiver.

STEP 1

Hold the ball to your chest with both hands. Your thumbs should be behind it and your fingers either side.

STEP 2

Grip the ball firmly and flex your wrists backwards. Step forwards and extend your arms sharply in the direction of the receiver.

STEP 3

As your arms straighten, release the ball firmly with a flick of the wrists. Your fingers should be pointing in the direction you want the ball to go, with your thumbs downwards.

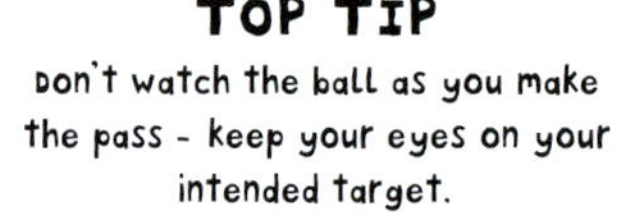

TOP TIP

Don't watch the ball as you make the pass - keep your eyes on your intended target.

OVERHEAD PASS

If you can't pass directly to a teammate because there is an opponent in the way, you may have to go over them. To do this, use the overhead pass.

STEP 1
Hold the ball above your head with your fingers cupping the underside of the ball, keeping it out of reach of your marker.

STEP 2
Release the ball just above your head, using a short, sharp flick of the wrists and a short forward movement of the arms. Make sure your eyes are on the intended target.

BOUNCE PASS
Another way to pass when you are tightly marked is with the bounce pass.

STEP 1
With your marker stretching his arms out to prevent the chest pass, bend your knees and extend your arm out to make the angle for the pass.

STEP 2
Bounce the ball to your teammate. Because the ball will slow down when it hits the floor, aim for the ball to hit the floor about two-thirds of the way to the receiver – this will reduce the chance of an interception.

ON THE COURT: PASSING

Become a pass master with the help of these great passing exercises and drills.

PIGGY IN THE MIDDLE (3 PLAYERS)

This is a classic drill; great for sharpening up those passing skills. It is good for working on 'piggy's' defensive play too.

WALL PASSING (1 PERSON)

STEP 1

Simply stand a few yards from the wall, and throw the ball against it. Imagine that you are passing the ball through the wall to someone opposite you.

STEP 1

Two players stand about 10 feet (3 meters) apart. They must pass the ball to each other, while a third (defensive) player stands between them and tries to block or intercept the ball.

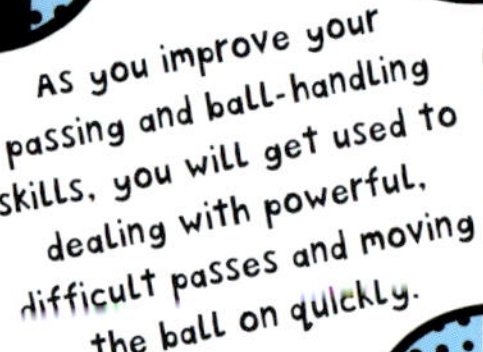

STEP 2

As the ball bounces back off the wall, catch it and repeat. Try to vary the passes, using a combination of chest, overhead and bounce passes.

STEP 2

When the player in the middle has touched the ball once, swap positions with a passing player.

TOP TIP

The passing players should not use overhead passes as it makes it too easy to bypass the 'piggy'.

TWO-PLAYER PASSING DRILL

This is a great drill for improving your passing and catching under pressure.

STEP 1

Two players line up opposite each other, about 10 feet (3 meters) apart, both with basketballs in their hands. On the call of three, each player must pass the ball to the player opposite.

STEP 2

One player must play a chest pass while the other plays a bounce pass . As soon as the players catch the ball, they should pass it back immediately, maintaining a constant, fast-moving drill.

MACHINE GUN PASSING (5 PLAYERS)

In a game of basketball the action comes thick and fast, which is why this lightning-quick passing drill is so useful.

STEP 1

Stand four players in a semicircle, all facing a fifth player (player A) who stands about 8 feet (2.5 meters) away. Player A has a basketball in his hands, as does one of the players in the semicircle, player B.

STEP 2

After the whistle, player A passes the ball quickly to one of the players in the semicircle, calling out the name of the intended receiver. As soon as the ball has been released, player B quickly passes his ball to player A. Player A receives it, then passes it to another player in the semicircle. This cycle continues in quick, rapid-fire succession requiring good reactions and concentration.

SHOOTING

Anyone in a team can score a goal, so perfecting your shooting techniques is vital for scoring points.

THE SET SHOT

The set shot is used when you are standing still, relatively close to the basket. It is also the kind of shot you would use for a free throw.

STEP 1
From a standing position with your knees slightly apart, crouch down facing the basket. If you are shooting with your right hand, your right leg should be slightly further forward than your left.

STEP 2
With your non-shooting hand gripping the side of the ball and your shooting hand facing towards the basket, begin to straighten your legs and spring up towards the basket.

STEP 3
Lift yourself up on to your toes in one movement. Use your non-shooting hand to steady the ball, then shoot with a strong flick of the wrist.

THE JUMP SHOT

Often the only way to get your shot past an opponent in front of you is to jump and release the ball in midair.

STEP 1
With your feet flat on the floor facing the basket, crouch down low to give you enough force to jump off the ground.

STEP 2
Straighten up, bringing the ball into the shooting position as you rise with the elbow of your shooting arm directly beneath the ball.

STEP 3
Spring off the ground to shoot above the reach of any defender. Focus on the basket as you release the ball.

THE LAY-UP SHOT

Unlike the previous two shots, the lay-up is used when you are on the move. It is all about driving right to the basket and using the backboard to help you score.

STEP 1

Approach the basket from the side as you dribble towards it. Put all your weight on your front leg – if you are right-handed then this should be your left leg – and bend your knee to give you the spring to jump.

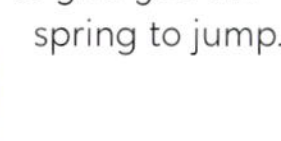

STEP 2

Spring off your forward leg, raising your arms ready to throw the ball.

STEP 3

Jump up towards the basket (go up to the side of it, not directly in front of the hoop). As you reach the top of your jump, transfer the ball to your shooting hand, extend your arm as far as it will go and release the ball.

STEP 4

The ball should bounce off the backboard and go softly into the hoop.

TOP TIP

Aim for the small rectangle on the backboard. The perfect shot should hit the top corner of the rectangle, on your side of the basket.

ON THE COURT: SHOOTING

It is crucial that when you get a shooting chance in a basketball match you make it count, because if you miss, your team may well lose the ball. That is why – even for top players – it is crucial to practice shooting.

ONE-PLAYER DRILL

Stand close to the basket and practice set shots and jump shots from the same point.

Keep shooting until you can get five of each in a row, then move to another spot. Move farther out from the basket or change your angle. Try shooting with both hands, too.

AROUND THE WORLD (1-2 PLAYERS)

This drill teaches you to vary your shooting distance and angle around the basket.

Stand on one of the marks on the key closest to the basket and shoot. If you score, fetch the ball and move onto the next mark. If you miss, remain on your spot until the next go. See how quickly you can go around the key from 1 to 10, scoring baskets (including the free throw line and a field goal position on the outside of the key). Set a record, then try to beat it!

TOP TIP

Try racing a friend. This added pressure teaches you to get into position and shoot quickly, just as you would have to do in a match situation.

LAY-UP DRILL

Keep things moving with this lay-up shooting drill, which also provides rebounding and passing practice.

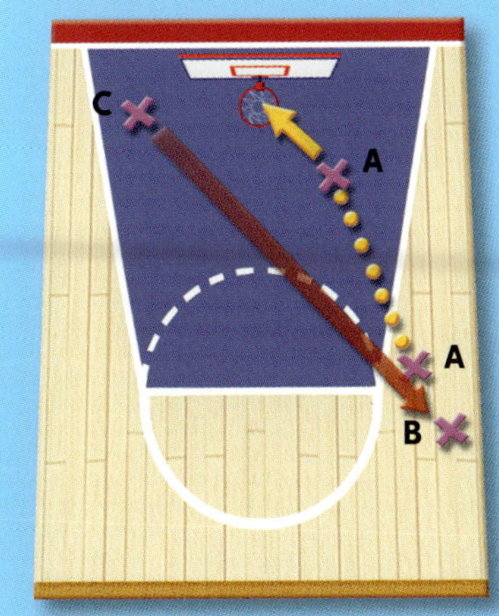

Two players (A and B) stand on the edge of the key to the right of the basket, while a third (player C) stands just to the left of the basket. Player A approaches the basket and attempts a lay-up shot. Player C collects the ball and passes it back to player B at the edge of the key. Player B now runs at the basket, while player A moves under the basket to replace player C. Player C moves to the edge to receive and immediately play the ball. The cycle continues.

This is another fast-moving drill involving three players – two providers and one shooter. It allows the shooter to get into a good rhythm.

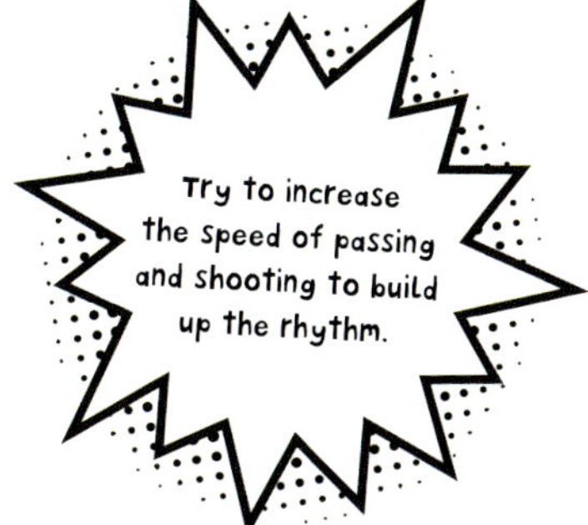

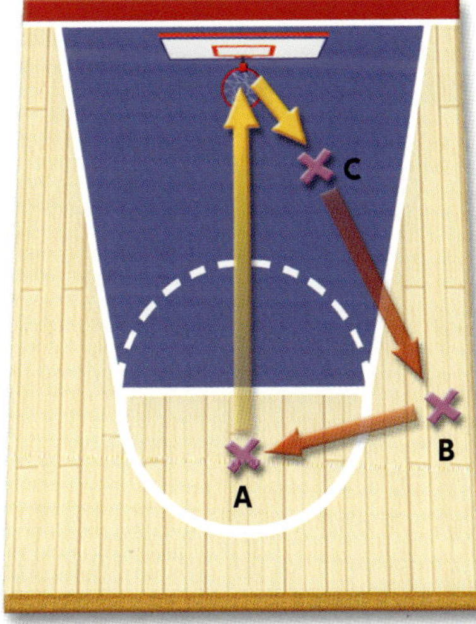

The shooter (player A) stands on the edge of the key. Player B stands on the other side of the key and player C waits under the basket. Player A shoots, player C collects the ball and passes it quickly to player B. Player B passes it swiftly on to player A who shoots again. When player A has five attempts, all the players move round one position and the drill starts again.

THE REBOUND

When someone takes a shot, there's a good chance that it will bounce off the backboard or the hoop. This is called a rebound, and winning the ball from this situation is a crucial part of the game.

BOXING OUT

When a player shoots, you must attempt to put yourself between the basket and your opponent. This is called boxing out, and is used to win the rebound.

STEP 1

As the shot is made, anticipate a rebound by positioning your body between the hoop and your marker.

STEP 2

Watching the ball at all times, bend your knees and spread out your arms, making your body big and strong. Get ready to jump up as it rebounds.

TIPPING-IN

If you are on the attack near the hoop and you judge the rebound perfectly, rather than catching the ball and then having a shot you can try to tip the ball straight back into the basket without landing. Be warned, though, this is tough!

Tipping-in is a very difficult skill to perfect, and requires good judgement and a spectacular jump. As you watch the flight of the shot, anticipate the rebound and launch yourself into the air just as the ball hits the rim or the backboard. Adjust your body in mid-air and try to get a hand to it. If you can get there, try to guide the ball into the basket with a gentle flick of the hand.

TOP TIP

The secret of tipping-in is to guide the ball into the basket, not shoot it in. Usually it will only require the lightest of touches to guide the bouncing ball back into the basket.

DEFENSIVE CATCHING

As a defender, if you catch a rebound from an opposition shot, you regain possession for your team, which turns your defense instantly into an attack.

STEP 1

By boxing out your opponent, you have made yourself favorite to win the ball if it rebounds. When it does, aim to catch it at the highest point possible. Doing this is all about timing your jump. Don't jump too early or you may find yourself on the way down as the ball reaches catching height.

STEP 2

As you catch the ball, turn away from your nearest opponent so that the ball is shielded as you land.

OFFENSIVE CATCHING

It is just as crucial for attacking players to follow up on rebounds as it is for defenders. Regaining control of the ball means the attack stays alive and you or your team may still score.

Just like defensive catching, the secret to successful offensive rebound play is position, anticipation and timing. Try to outfox the defensive marker who is trying to block you by faking to move one way then darting the other. Try and get yourself into the boxing out position so that you are better placed to time your jump and win the ball. If you win the ball and have enough space, jump straight back up and shoot!

ON THE COURT: REBOUNDING

It may be more fun to practice shooting and dribbling, but rebounding is so crucial to the game of basketball that it is important to find time to sharpen up your play.

ONE-PLAYER DRILL

STEP 1

Stand under the basket, 5 feet (1.5 meters) away from the baseline, and shoot the ball against the backboard.

STEP 2

As the ball rebounds, jump and catch it. Work on timing your leap so that you jump forward to meet the ball, catching it at the highest point you can.

TIPPING-IN DRILL (2-10 PLAYERS)

A line of players, each with a ball, stands outside the key, to one side of the free throw line. One by one they pass their ball to a player standing on the free throw line who shoots at the backboard so that the ball rebounds. The player who has passed the ball follows up on the shot, jumps and tries to tip the ball directly in. Then he collects his ball and goes to the back of the line while the next player begins the routine. If the rebound cannot be tipped-in, catch it and shoot.

ONE-ON-ONE REBOUND DRILL (3 PLAYERS)

Two opposing players (A and B) stand in the center of the key, 6 feet (1.8 meters) away from the basket. While they try to block each other out, a third player (C) shoots at the backboard from the free throw line. Players A and B must compete to catch the rebound. Adjust the drill by making A an attacking player and B defensive. While A must try to tip-in or shoot from the rebound, B must try to catch the ball or block A's attempts at scoring. For a further progression add two more players, one attacking and one defending, to recreate a match-type rebound situation.

PROGRESSION 1

Adjust the drill by making A an attacking player and B defensive. While A must try to tip-in or shoot from the rebound, B must try to catch the ball or block A's attempts at scoring.

PROGRESSION 2

For a further progression add two more players, one attacking and one defending, to recreate a match-type rebound situation.

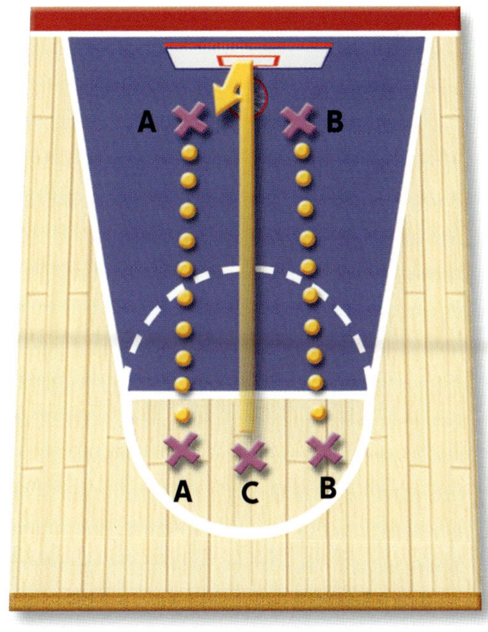

DEFENDING

Just as every player on a basketball team must be able to pass and shoot, every player must also be able to get behind the ball and defend when the other team is in possession.

DEFENSIVE STANCE

When you are facing an opponent who has the ball, you must take up a position that makes it difficult to pass or shoot. Bend your knees and stay on your toes so that you can react quickly. Standing with one arm raised and one arm lowered, with both hands open, allows you to prevent both a chest and a bounce pass.

PREVENTING PASS RECEPTION

If you are marking a player who is ready to receive the ball, position yourself alongside your opponent so that you can get your arm across to prevent the pass. Your opponent will try to move away from you, so stay on your toes and keep close without obstructing your opponent.

DEFENSE AGAINST A DRIBBLER

STEP 1

Get your body between the ball and the basket and take up the defensive stance, then move with your opponent as they dribble. Don't get too close, as a quick burst of speed or a side-step will beat you. Just try to block your opponent's path, forcing them away from the basket.

STEP 2

Bend your knees and keep your feet flat on the floor, then by shuffling, rather than taking steps, you can quickly react to your opponent's changes of speed and direction.

MARKING A PASSER

When your opponent has the ball, you should make it as hard as possible for him to pass it on to a teammate.

STEP 1

Adopt the defensive stance and keep on your toes, so that you can react to your opponent's moves and fakes.

STEP 2

Use your arms and hands to block any attempt at passing or shooting.

Be aggressive and physical, without actually touching your opponent. If you do, a foul will be awarded against you. The secret of great defending is to use your brain as well as your body. If you anticipate your opponent's next move, you will know how to stop it.

TOP TIP

You must be aware of the movement of both the passer and the pass receiver, so keep both of them in your sight.

ON THE COURT: DEFENDING

It is important that basketball players work on their defensive game and here are some drills that can make it fun.

ZIGZAG (2 PLAYERS)

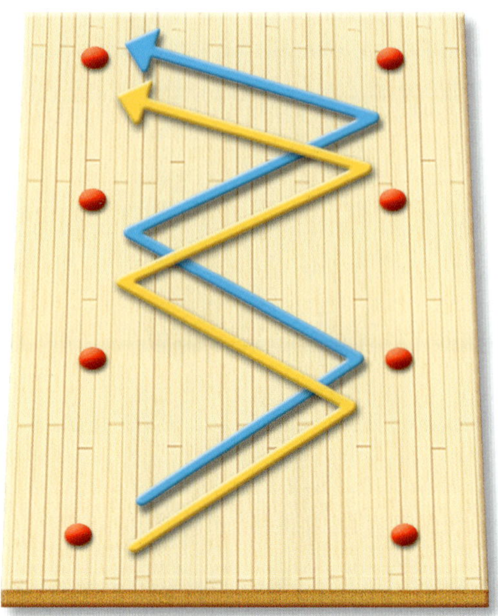

Mark out an area of about 12 feet (3.5 meters) wide and about half a court long. An offensive player must dribble the entire length of this line, keeping the ball alive within the marked out area and traveling in a zigzag pattern. At the same time, a defensive player tracks this dribble, attempting to disrupt his opponent and/or steal the ball.

DENIAL DRILL (3 PLAYERS)

This drill requires two offensive players and a defensive player whose role it is to try and prevent pass reception. One offensive player with the ball stands about 16 feet (5 meters) from the other. The defensive player must try to get in front of the pass receiver, moving constantly to make it difficult for the pass to get through.

TOP TIP

If you are defending, try to be roughly two steps in front of your opponent (towards the passer) and only one step away from the line of the intended pass.

TWO-ON-TWO PLAY

Playing two-on-two basketball is a great way to develop all the skills required in the game of basketball – from dribbling and shooting to passing and rebounding. It is a particularly good drill for improving your defending as you are under serious pressure when you or your teammate do not have the ball.

STEP 1

Two teams of two players play a mini game of basketball in which they both score in the same basket. All players stay within the area of the key. The game is started from the free throw line and, if one team scores or puts the ball out of play, the other team restarts.

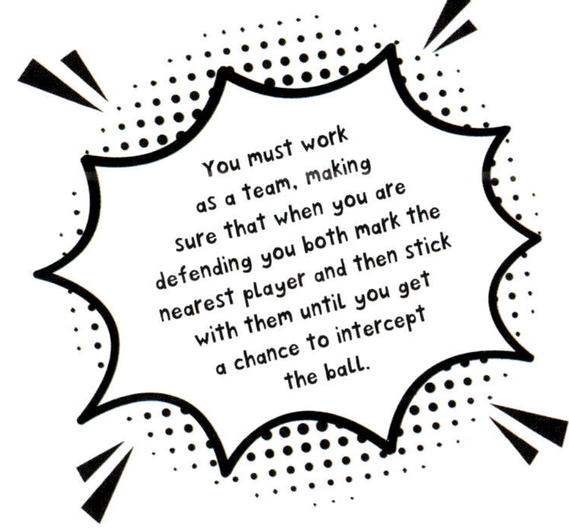

STEP 2

When the other team has the ball, you can see what a difference good defensive play makes. If you lose your concentration and your position for a second, you will give the opposition a chance to score.

ADVANCED DRIBBLING

Now you have mastered the basics, it is time to get flash! You should now feel comfortable enough with the basketball in your hands to try the techniques of pro players.

ADVANCE DRIBBLING

If you run in a straight line, dribbling the ball with the same hand, it is easier for a defending opponent to block your path or steal the ball. If you switch hands, or bounce the ball between your legs and behind your back, it gives the opposition little chance to gain possession.

CROSSOVER DRIBBLING

STEP 1
As you dribble forwards, keep your legs apart and your body low. Bring the ball to your side.

STEP 2
Still moving forward, bounce the ball across the front of your body and into your other hand.

STEP 3
Immediately bounce the ball back to the other hand, continuing your forward motion.

BETWEEN THE LEGS DRIBBLING

STEP 1
As you dribble, step forward, bringing the ball to your side.

STEP 2
Allow the ball to bounce out to your side, giving you room to take another step forward.

STEP 3
Bounce the ball back through your legs – making the gap as wide as you can and guiding the ball cleanly through it – to your other hand again.

STEP 4
Bounce the ball sideways between the gap in your legs, bringing your receiving hand down to collect it.

BEHIND THE BACK DRIBBLING

STEP 1
With your legs wide apart and body position low, bring the ball out to your side.

STEP 2
Looking straight ahead, bounce the ball gently behind you. Bring your other hand behind your back to receive it.

STEP 3
As the ball touches your receiving hand, bring your arm up with the bounce and out to the side of your body.

STEP 4
Using the palm of your hand on the top of the ball, ease it back the other way, as before.

TIP OFF

A basketball game is started and restarted (after each quarter and some fouls) with a jump ball. Win the ball and put your team in the driving seat.

JUMP BALL

The referee throws the ball up between two players in the center circle. They must jump up and try to tip it to their teammates. The two players must not touch the ball until it reaches its highest point, and can only touch it twice. After that it must only be touched by another player.

STEP 1

Crouch opposite your opponent, with your body weight over your toes so that you can easily spring up to the ball when it comes into play.

Be careful not to jump too soon. If you do, you will be on the way back down at the point where you should be at the top of your jump and you will miss the ball!

STEP 2

As the ball is played into the air, time your jump so that you meet the ball at its highest point. Watch the ball as you jump, extending your body and your arms so that you are at full stretch when it starts to come down. If you make it to the ball first, try to tip it to your teammates who are waiting around the edge of the center circle.

ADVANCED SHOOTING

If you pull off a hook shot or a slam dunk, not only will your team be two points up but you'll be king of the court!

THE HOOK SHOT

When the direct route to the basket is blocked, the hook shot can be the only way to get in a shot on the basket.

STEP 1

Move away from your marker by pivoting. Keep your back turned on your opponent to protect the ball.

STEP 2

As you turn, transfer the ball to your shooting hand and cup it with your outstretched fingers. Extend your arm straight out behind you as you lift your back leg off the ground.

STEP 3

As you spring off your forward leg, keep your arm straight and the ball cupped in your shooting hand. Bowl the ball over your head towards the hoop. Release the ball at full stretch and at the top of your jump.

THE SLAM DUNK

The slam dunk is the most famous shot in basketball because it is the most spectacular. However, you must either be very tall or a superb jumper to pull it off.

STEP 1

Approach the basket running as fast as you can, springing off on your left leg if you have the ball in your right hand (and vice versa).

STEP 2

You need to jump high enough to get the whole ball over the height of the hoop.

STEP 3

If you have gone high enough, you will literally be able to slam the ball down into the basket.

WARMING UP & STRETCHING

Warming up and stretching before a training session or a match is very important. It lessens the chances of injury and increases a player's speed and ability to twist and turn.

WARMING UP

Before you pick up a ball or even begin stretching, it is important to warm up your body. This dramatically lessens your chance of pulling a muscle or a tendon (the cause of more than half of all soccer injuries). All you need to do is a light jog for five minutes. This will increase your heart rate and get the blood pumping around your body.

STRETCHING

You must be very careful with your stretching.

- **Never stretch until the body is warmed up.**
- **Always stretch slowly and gently and never so much that it is uncomfortable.**
- **Hold each stretch for 10 to 20 seconds, keeping your body steady at all times.**
- **Never rock or bounce on a stretch.**
- **Breathe out as you stretch.**
- **Stretch both before and after exercise.**

There are many stretches, but here are some of the most important. Ask a coach or a physiotherapist to show you others, and check that you are doing them correctly.

TOUCH YOUR TOES

Gently bend down as if you were going to touch your toes, but stop when you feel tension in the back of your legs. Hold the stretch for 10 seconds and then try reaching down a little more. Slowly you should be able to reach further and further until you can actually get right down.

CALF STRETCH

Put the weight of your body on the front foot, bending the knee and stretching the other leg behind with the weight resting on your toes. Then lean forward so that your hands touch the ground, and slowly push your outstretched leg back.

GROIN STRETCH

Stand with your legs apart. Then, placing one hand on your thigh, dip your shoulder and lean to one side until you feel slight tension in your groin muscles on that side. Hold the stretch there, then repeat on the other side.

HAMSTRING STRETCH

Lie on your back, and gently lift one leg up in the air. Use your hands to keep the leg straight until you feel tension in your hamstrings at the back of your leg. Hold the stretch there, then repeat with the other leg.

TWO'S COMPANY

Some stretches can be done with a teammate. This develops better balance. Keep the stretch steady and safe.

DIET

You can't make yourself more skillful by consuming certain foods, but you can give yourself more energy and stamina on the court by eating a well balanced diet.

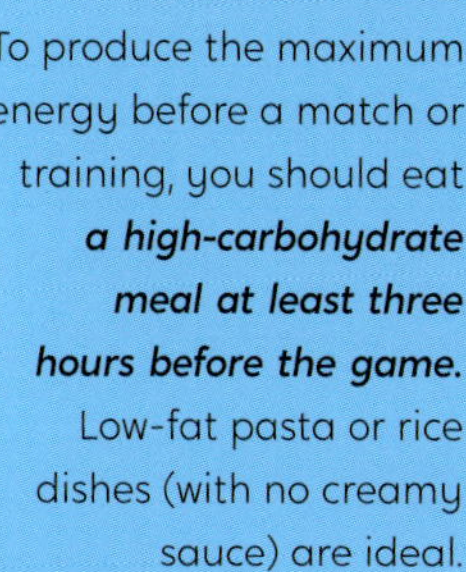

ENERGY BUSTERS

If you are doing a lot of exercise, then you need to eat plenty of *carbohydrates* to provide the energy for the exercise you are doing.

Protein is required for the growth and repair of the body, but try to choose low-fat sources, since some fatty foods can cause stomach discomfort if eaten before exercising.

BEFORE THE MATCH

To produce the maximum energy before a match or training, you should eat *a high-carbohydrate meal at least three hours before the game.* Low-fat pasta or rice dishes (with no creamy sauce) are ideal.

In the run-up to the game, *boost your carbohydrate levels with fast-digesting snacks, such as bananas or dried fruit.*

It is crucial to *drink plenty of liquid before a game*. Water or isotonic sports drinks consumed two or three hours before playing will make up for the water you lose (through sweat) when playing.

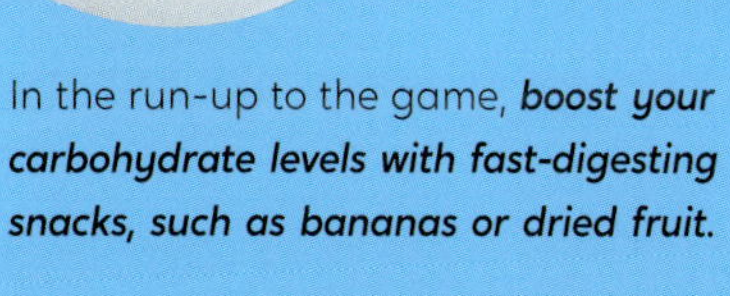

MENTAL ATTITUDE

As well as preparing the body, it is also important to prepare the mind for a basketball match and even training. Much of the skill of being a good basketball player is to do it with confidence and self-belief. If you believe you will score you most likely will.

MENTAL PREPARATION

More and more sports coaches are using methods of coaching that focus on the psychological side as well as the physical. Pro basketball clubs will often use a sports psychologist to work with the players on their positive thinking and concentration, as well as building up faith in themselves and their teammates.

Basketball is such a quick game that it is essential not to lose concentration for a moment – during that moment you might lose your opponent or fumble the ball. Try to focus all the time, never letting your mind drift from the game for even a second. Some teams also like to focus together, gathering into a huddle before the match or at the end of a time-out. Basketball is a team game, and it is important that the team is together. If you are, and you believe in each other, you will be more prepared to run yourself through the pain barrier for your teammates and they will be prepared to do the same.

GLOSSARY

Basket The hoop and net through which the ball must go to record a score. Also the name for a score.

Backboard The rectangle behind the basket, off which the ball is allowed to rebound.

Boxing out The positioning of a player between the basket and an opponent to win a rebound.

Bounce pass A pass where the ball is bounced off the ground to a teammate.

Chest pass A short, direct pass made at chest height.

Court The playing area for a basketball match.

Defense When a team has the ball, the other team is on defense to try and stop them scoring.

Dribbling Moving around the court whilst dribbling the ball. .

Fake When a player pretends to move or throw the ball one way, but stops an goes the other to fool an opponent.

Field goal A basket scored, with the exception of free throws, from anywhere on the three point line.

Foul An illegal play.

Free throw An unopposed shot, taken from behind the free throw line and awarded after an opposing foul.

Hook shot A shot where the ball is played over a players' head from alongside the basket.

Hoop The circular section of the basket which the ball must go through to score.

Jump ball Used to start and restart the game, with two opposing players jumping against each other to win a ball thrown by the referee.

Jump shot A shot played while the shooter is jumping in the air.

Key The restricted area underneath the basket at each end.

Lay-up shot When you take one and a half steps towards the net and shoot the ball off the backborad into the basket.

NBA National Basketball Association.

Offense When a team is in possession of the ball, they are on offense and trying to score.

Overhead pass A pass to a teammate played above the head.

Overtime An extra period of five minutes played if the scores are level at full-time.

Pivoting Turning on the spot while holding the ball.

Rebound A shot that misses the basket and bounces back off the hoop or backboard.

Referee The official in charge of a basketball match. At the top level there may be more than one referee in a match.

Set shot A straight shot at the basket, taken with both feet on the ground.

Slam dunk A shot where the ball is held above the basket and then forced downwards through it.

Steal Legally gaining possession of the ball from a dribbler or passer.

Three-pointer See 'Field goal'.

Throw-in A free throw from the sideline.

Time-out A one-minute break in play called by the coach.

Tip-in A shot where the ball is rebounded off the backboard into the basket.

Triple threat position The standard position to protect the ball, adopted when players receive the ball.

INDEX